JOHN RUTTER

WINCHESTER TE DEUM

FOR MIXED VOICES AND ORGAN,
ORGAN WITH BRASS ENSEMBLE,
OR ORCHESTRA

MUSIC DEPARTMENT

OXFORD
UNIVERSITY PRESS

OXFORD

UNIVERSITY PRESS

Great Clarendon Street, Oxford OX2 6DP, England
198 Madison Avenue, New York, NY 10016, USA

Oxford University Press is a department of the University of Oxford.
It furthers the University's aim of excellence in research, scholarship,
and education by publishing worldwide in

Oxford New York
Auckland Cape Town Hong Kong Karachi
Kuala Lumpur Madrid Melbourne Mexico City Nairobi
New Delhi Shanghai Taipei Toronto

With offices in

Argentina Austria Brazil Chile Czech Republic France Greece
Guatemala Hungary Italy Japan Poland Portugal Singapore
South Korea Switzerland Thailand Turkey Ukraine Vietnam

Oxford is a registered trade mark of Oxford University Press
in the UK and in certain other countries

10

ISBN 978-0-19-335689-4

Printed in Great Britain on acid-free paper by
Halstan & Co. Ltd., Amersham, Bucks.

INSTRUMENTATION

The accompaniment to this work exists in three versions:

1. For organ alone. The organist plays from the vocal score.

2. For organ with five-part brass ensemble (2 trumpets in B flat, horn in F, trombone, and tuba), plus optional timpani (1 player) and optional percussion (2 players). The organist plays from the full score.

3. For full orchestra (without organ).

Full scores and instrumental parts for versions 2 and 3 are available on hire from the publisher. Please specify, when ordering, which version is required.

Duration: 7–8 minutes

Winchester Te Deum

JOHN RUTTER

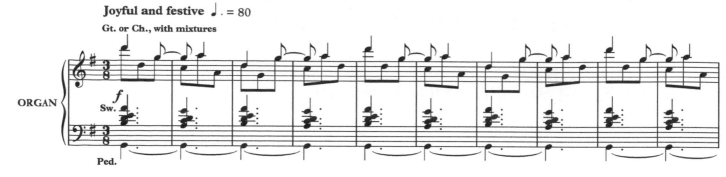

thee:_____ the Fa - ther____ ev - er - last - ing,____ the Fa - - - ther ev - er -

-last - ing.___

To thee all an - gels cry a - loud:___ the hea - vens,___ the

To thee all an - gels cry a - loud:___ the

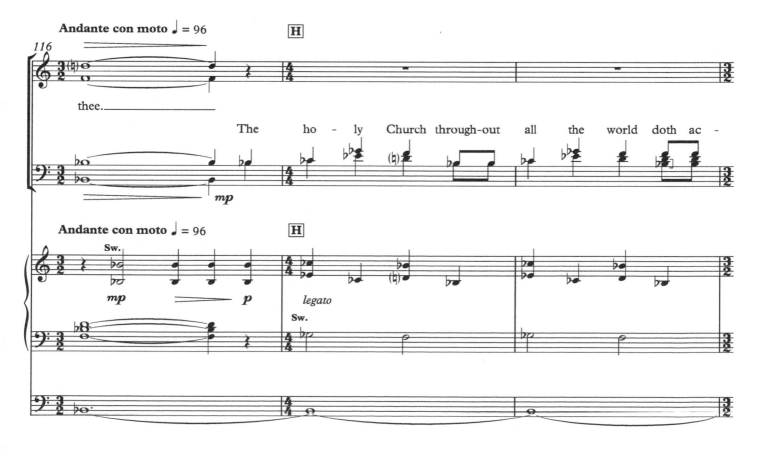

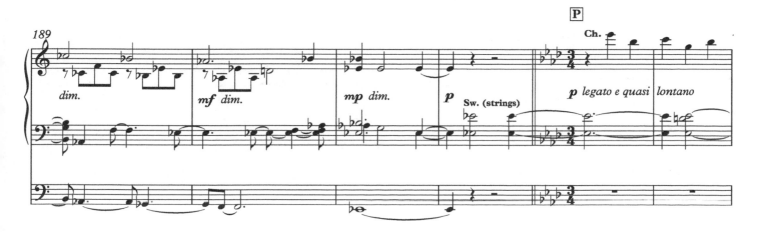

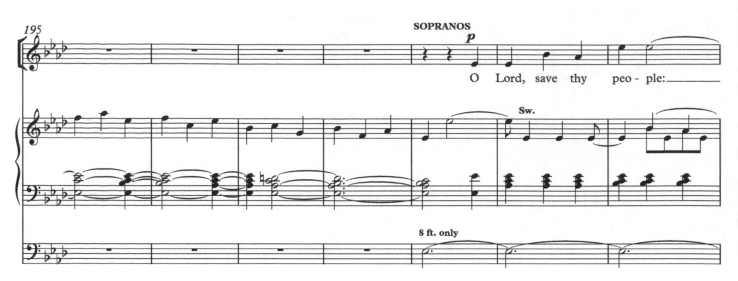

195 SOPRANOS *p*
O Lord, save thy peo - ple:

Sw.

8 ft. only

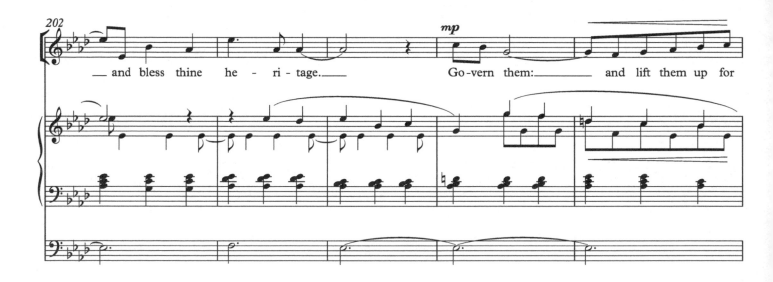

202 *mp*
and bless thine he - ri - tage. Go - vern them: and lift them up for

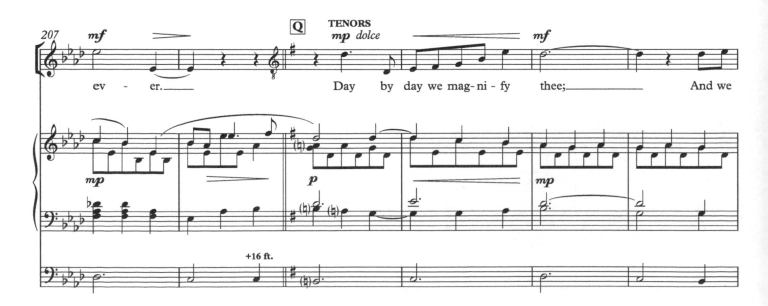

207 *mf* **Q** TENORS *mp dolce* *mf*
ev - er. Day by day we mag - ni - fy thee; And we

mp *p* *mp*

+16 ft.

SOPRANOS

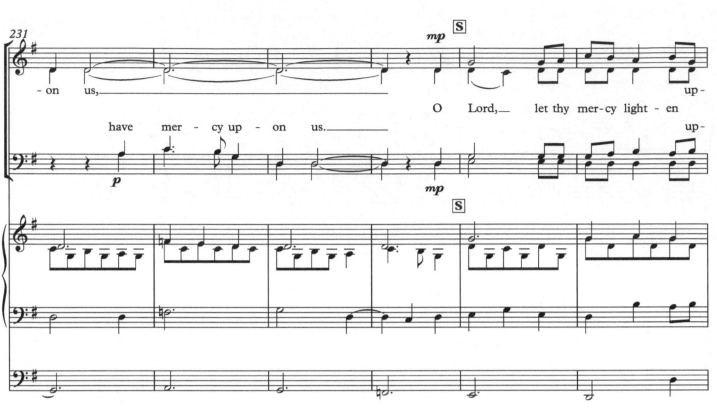